A DAY IN THE LIFE

Snakes

WHAT DO COBRAS, PYTHONS, AND
ANACONDAS GET UP TO ALL DAY?

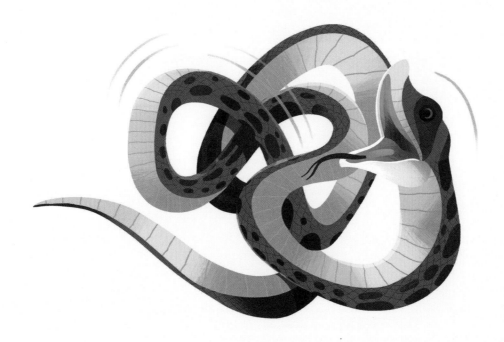

NEON SQUID

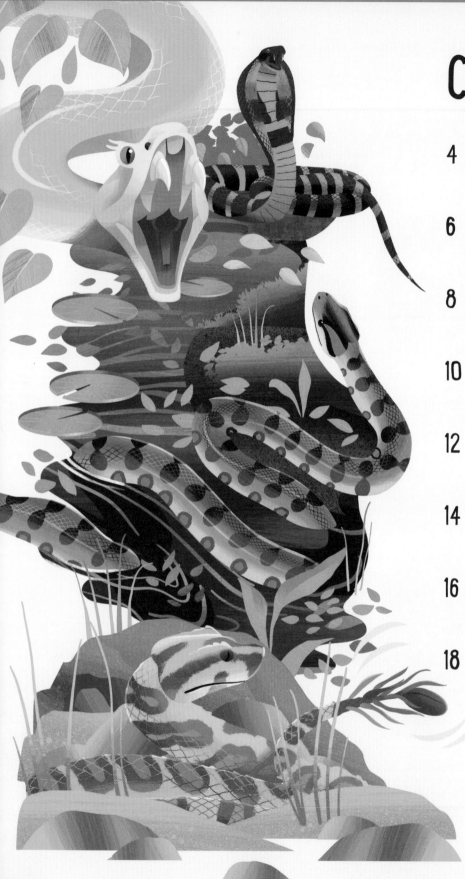

Contents

Welcome to the world of snakes!

For as long as I can remember, snakes have been feared and even hated by people around me. Growing up, I was told to stay away from snakes and that the only good snake is a dead one. Then, one day when I was eight years old, I had a life-changing experience with a black racer snake in my back garden. It stood up and **looked me right in the eyes**, but it didn't bite me like everyone said it would—it just slithered away!

From that day on I wanted to learn all about snakes. I read books and tried to encounter them in the wild as much as I could. This has led me to become a **wildlife educator**. My goal is to teach as many people as possible that snakes are amazing animals that deserve respect.

There are more than **3,000 species of snake** on Earth. Whether it's the Pacific Ocean, a blistering desert, snowy meadows in Norway, or your own back garden, you can find snakes almost everywhere! They range from the gigantic reticulated python, which grows as long as a minibus, to the tiny Barbados threadsnake that could fit in the palm of your hand. Snakes are truly spectacular and unique animals that play important roles in the ecosystems they inhabit. Let's meet some of them and discover what they get up to during a normal day in their lives!

Christian Cave

Snake anatomy

Snakes can be long or short, huge or tiny, and live in deserts, jungles, oceans, or high up in the trees. Even though there are many species of snakes, they all share some of the same features. Let's have a look at what makes these reptiles such fierce predators.

Skeleton

Snake skeletons are rather simple: they have a very long spine with many vertebrae and hundreds of ribs that guard the organs.

Tail

Believe it or not, even though its entire body is long and wiggly, a snake has a tail! It starts after its reproductive organs and has up to 205 spinal bones called vertebrae.

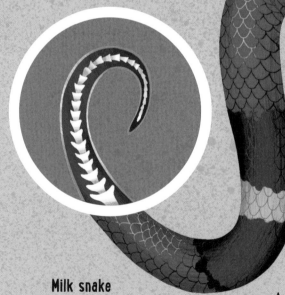

Milk snake

Scales

A snake's entire body is covered in scales—even its eyes! Scales, like human hair, are made of a substance called keratin. They reduce moisture loss and protect the snake.

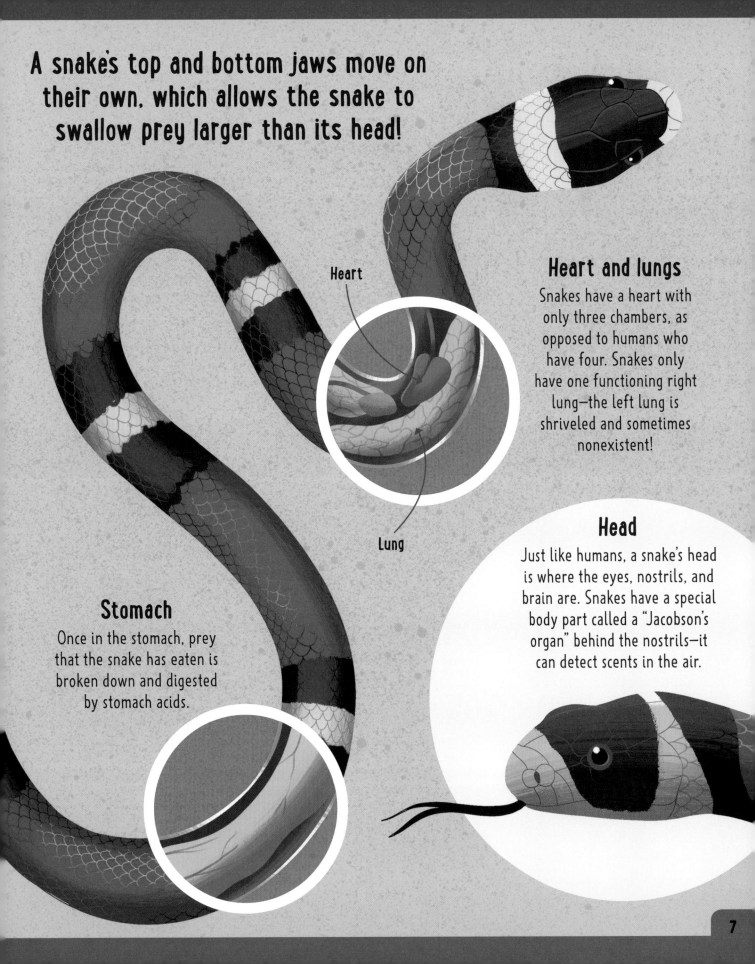

A snake's top and bottom jaws move on their own, which allows the snake to swallow prey larger than its head!

Heart

Lung

Heart and lungs

Snakes have a heart with only three chambers, as opposed to humans who have four. Snakes only have one functioning right lung—the left lung is shriveled and sometimes nonexistent!

Head

Just like humans, a snake's head is where the eyes, nostrils, and brain are. Snakes have a special body part called a "Jacobson's organ" behind the nostrils—it can detect scents in the air.

Stomach

Once in the stomach, prey that the snake has eaten is broken down and digested by stomach acids.

Soaking up the sunshine

It's a cool morning in Florida, USA, and the sun has just peeked over the horizon. The longest snake in North America, the eastern indigo snake, slithers out of the gopher tortoise burrow he has been keeping warm in during the previous cold months. Snakes are **ectotherms**, which means that their body temperature depends on their surroundings. Right now, that glorious sunshine is this snake's best friend—it's giving him the warmth he will need to do something that he's be waiting to do for a while now: shed his skin!

Reptiles regularly shed their skin as they get older, and snakes are no exception. Think of a snake's skin as a jacket that is covering their whole body. As they grow, that jacket becomes tight, sticky, and tough—no one wants that!

Do you notice this snake's **pale blue eyes?** That means he's ready to start shedding. But first, he needs to sunbathe for a couple of hours. Don't worry—we'll catch up with him later.

Snakes have scales over their eyes called eye caps that become milky blue during shedding.

8AM Follow that smell

In the wetlands in Brazil, South America, prowls the world's heaviest snake—a green anaconda! On land she is very slow, but she makes up for it by being a skilled swimmer.

In this **harsh environment**, hunting can be tricky. The anaconda can see well, but in these murky waters that is almost useless! This is where her special senses come in. The anaconda can smell with her **tongue**, so she flicks it out to point her in the direction of her next victim. She picks up the scent of a nearby caiman who isn't aware of the danger lurking nearby.

The anaconda can also pick up **vibrations** from the caiman through a special bone in her jaw. She can sense these vibrations in the air or through the ground. They're sent to her internal ears, which process them as sounds. The anaconda is able to hear and feel the caiman's movements as she starts following its trail. The hunt is on!

Green anacondas live in slow-moving waters like rivers, streams, wetlands, marshes, lakes, and swamps.

Snakes use sight, smell, and sense of vibration to move through the world.

Better safe than sorry

It's a humid morning in the rainforests of Malaysia, and a reticulated python (the world's longest snake) is making his way back to the **tree stump** where he hides during the day. He's almost home when suddenly he freezes. He flicks out his tongue and picks up an alarming scent. An Indochinese leopard is on the hunt nearby!

The python can't see the leopard very well in the dense jungle, but he has a special ability that helps him detect predators... heat pits! These are **sensory organs** found in the lip scales of some snakes. The pits help snakes sense the heat that warm-blooded animals give off. It's almost like having night vision but during the day! The python detects the heat coming from the leopard right outside his tree stump and ducks back in. Phew—disaster avoided! The python gets comfortable and prepares himself for a long nap. He will wake up at night, when it will be his turn to hunt.

10AM Underground treasures

It's a beautiful day in the dry sandhills of south Georgia, USA. Very few reptiles stay above ground in this area during hot months because temperatures can reach 90°F (32°C). To **escape the heat** (and hopefully find a tasty snack in the process), a pine snake has a sneaky strategy. He digs through the sand with a special large scale on his nose called a rostral scale. He then uses tunnels that have already been dug by pocket gophers. To many animals, these tunnels provide a cool home during the day. To the pine snake, they are a treasure chest full of delicious prey waiting to be eaten!

This pine snake hasn't had breakfast yet. We all know it's the most important meal of the day, so it's time to **start digging**. His supersensitive tongue picks up the scent of a pocket gopher, and he moves in its direction. When the snake is close enough, he lunges for it! The pocket gopher leaps out of the way just in time. Our hungry snake will have to keep looking for breakfast.

Meanwhile... A paradise flying snake is resting on a tree in the Indonesian jungle. But wait... what's that hovering above?

Pine snakes spend so much of their lives underground that they have earned the nickname "ghost of the sandhills."

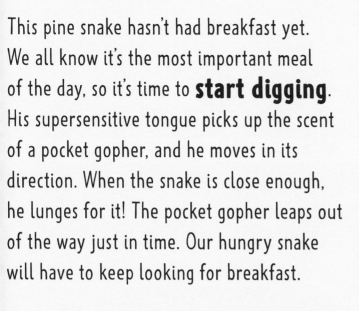

Pine snakes eat rodents, birds, lizards, eggs, and small mammals.

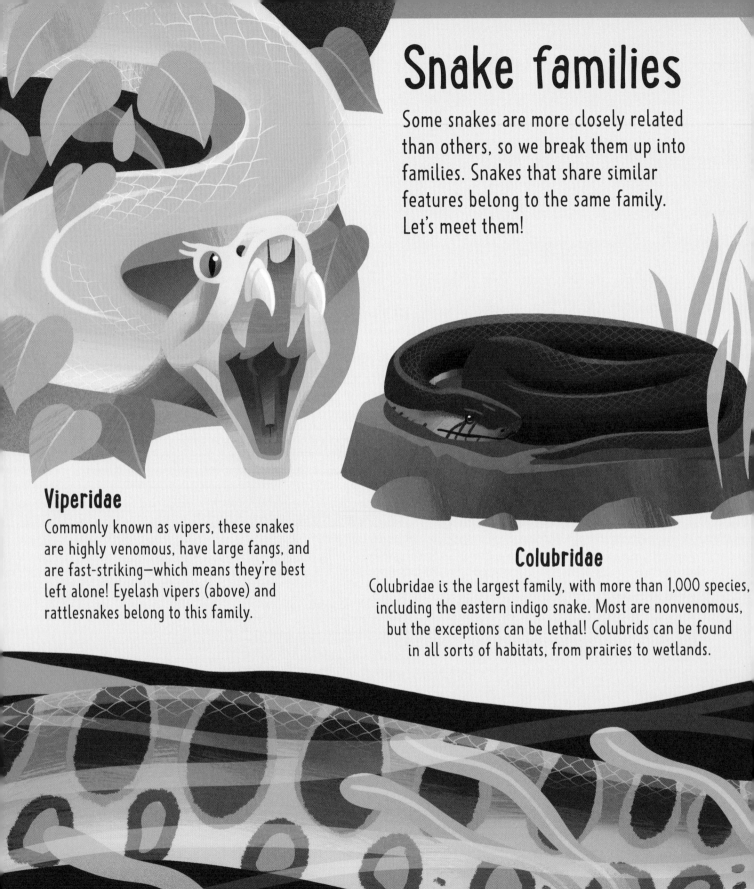

Snake families

Some snakes are more closely related than others, so we break them up into families. Snakes that share similar features belong to the same family. Let's meet them!

Viperidae

Commonly known as vipers, these snakes are highly venomous, have large fangs, and are fast-striking—which means they're best left alone! Eyelash vipers (above) and rattlesnakes belong to this family.

Colubridae

Colubridae is the largest family, with more than 1,000 species, including the eastern indigo snake. Most are nonvenomous, but the exceptions can be lethal! Colubrids can be found in all sorts of habitats, from prairies to wetlands.

Pythonidae

Members of the python family are nonvenomous, muscular snakes. Pythons lay eggs, and they are some of the largest snakes on the planet!

Elapidae

The most venomous snakes in the world are elapids—including the king cobra! Unlike vipers, their fangs do not fold.

Snakes are found all over the world, except in Antarctica.

Boidae

Boas are muscular snakes found primarily in the Americas. They are nonvenomous and give birth to live young. Some boas, such as anacondas, are fantastic swimmers.

A tight squeeze

Our green anaconda relies on stealth to get close to her prey and **ambush** it. Remember when she started following a caiman? Well, she's now ready to attack and plans to give it a big hug! But it's not as friendly as it sounds... The anaconda sneaks up on the caiman and in a flash wraps her muscular body around it, holding it very tight.

Every time the caiman breathes out, the anaconda tightens her squeeze, which makes its airway tighter and narrower. It's like trying to breathe through a small straw. Eventually, the caiman takes its last breath and dies. This method of killing prey is called **constriction** and many snakes use it, especially pythons and boas. It allows them to take down huge animals—after all, this caiman is the length of a small car! The anaconda then swallows the caiman headfirst. She must now find a safe place to digest her meal.

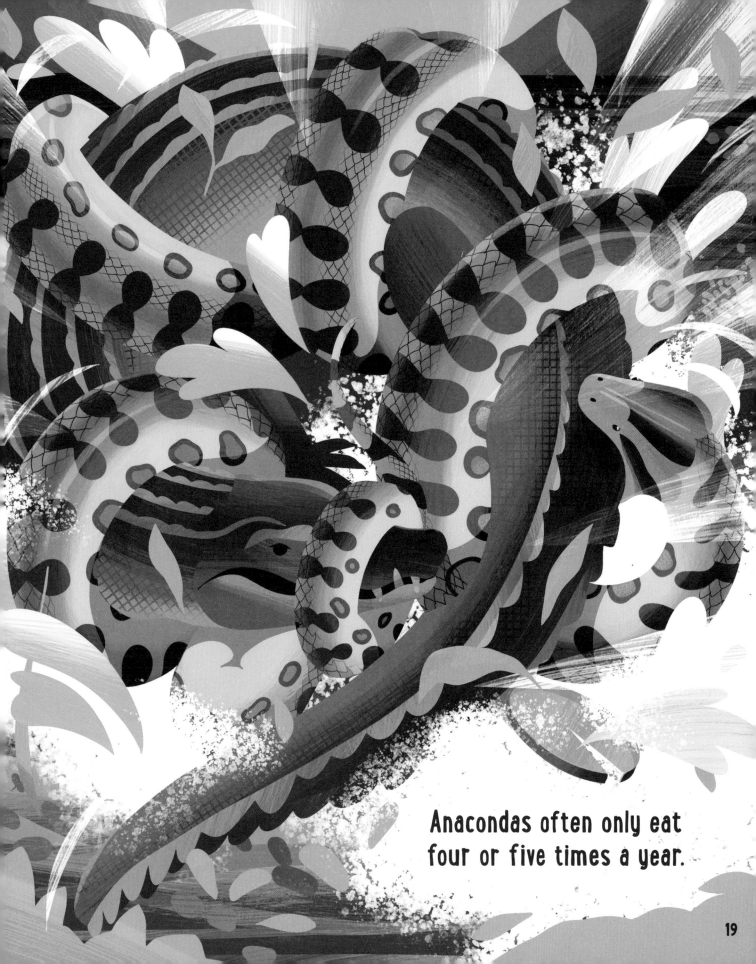

Anacondas often only eat
four or five times a year.

Venomous snakes shed their fangs periodically throughout their lives!

Hunting on the plains

It's midday on the sweltering, dry plains of Australia, where food and water is hard to come by. Most animals could not survive in this climate, so the ones that do are exceptionally good at catching or finding food! The **world's most venomous snake**, the inland taipan, is an example of both.

Like all taipans, he is equipped with extremely toxic venoms because he can't afford to let his prey escape—he'll never know when he might get his next meal! This taipan peeks down into the cracks of the dry soil and finds a plains rat who is **hiding** from the brutal Australian sun.

The rat makes a run for it, but the snake catches up to it and in one swift move chomps down! The snake's fangs, as sharp as doctor's needles, immediately deliver the venom. The venom paralyzes the small animal, making it unable to move. The taipan is in luck— lunch is served!

Meanwhile... In Virginia, USA, two male timber rattlesnakes encounter each other while looking for a pretty lady! The problem is, she'll only choose one...

Protecting the nest

It's a sunny afternoon in a rainforest in India, and a king cobra is busy keeping guard of her precious eggs. It won't be long until they hatch. The mother's nest lies at the base of a tree, and she has used dry leaf litter to create a warm and secure place for her eggs.

Suddenly, the mother **senses danger...** She spots a sneaky mongoose who is hoping to eat her eggs. There's no way she's letting that happen—her babies are relying on her for protection! As the mongoose approaches, the king cobra rears up and spreads a **wide hood** on her neck, making her look a lot bigger. She also has a venom that is strong enough to kill elephants, but luckily she won't need to use that today. The mongoose is frightened by her display and runs away. What a relief! The king cobra and her eggs are safe.

King cobras are
the longest venomous
snakes on Earth.

Out with the old

Now that the sun has warmed him up, our eastern indigo snake has to completely get rid of the **old skin** covering his body so that his new scales can come out, and he can't wait!

He's no newbie to this—the eastern indigo snake has shed his skin before and he will do so again many times in the future as he grows. Shedding, or **ecdysis**, is important for snakes because it allows them to grow and rids them of parasites. The new scales are also better at keeping moisture inside the snake, which is important when the weather is dry.

Scrittttttttt

The snake removes old skin from his head first so he can see.

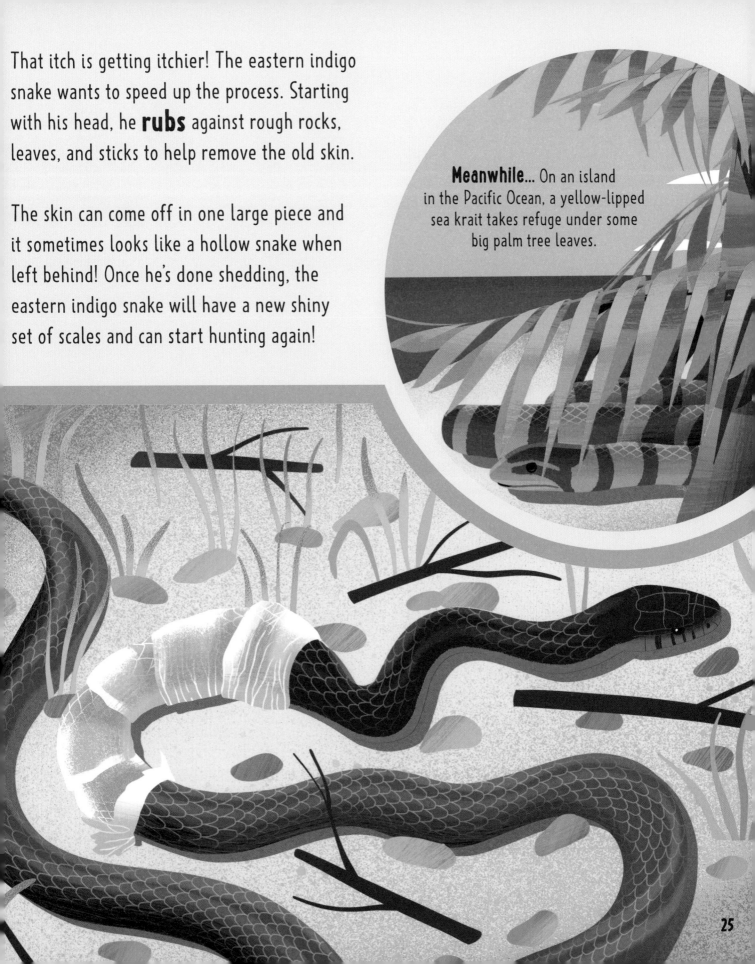

That itch is getting itchier! The eastern indigo snake wants to speed up the process. Starting with his head, he **rubs** against rough rocks, leaves, and sticks to help remove the old skin.

The skin can come off in one large piece and it sometimes looks like a hollow snake when left behind! Once he's done shedding, the eastern indigo snake will have a new shiny set of scales and can start hunting again!

Meanwhile... On an island in the Pacific Ocean, a yellow-lipped sea krait takes refuge under some big palm tree leaves.

Venomous or nonvenomous?

Some snakes have powerful venom, which they use to help them catch prey and protect themselves from predators. Out of nearly 4,000 snake species, around 600 are venomous. This means that seeing nonvenomous snakes is more common, but you should learn the differences between the two to be on the safe side. And remember: if you see a snake, it's best to keep your distance!

Round snout

Teeth

Teeth vs. fangs
Nonvenomous snakes have sharp teeth, but only venomous snakes have fangs that can inject venom.

Similar appearances
At first glance, venomous and nonvenomous snakes can look similar. They can be thin, chunky, long, or short.

Belly scales
Venomous and nonvenomous snakes have slightly different scales on their bellies. Venomous snakes have a single row and nonvenomous snakes have two rows.

Nonvenomous snake

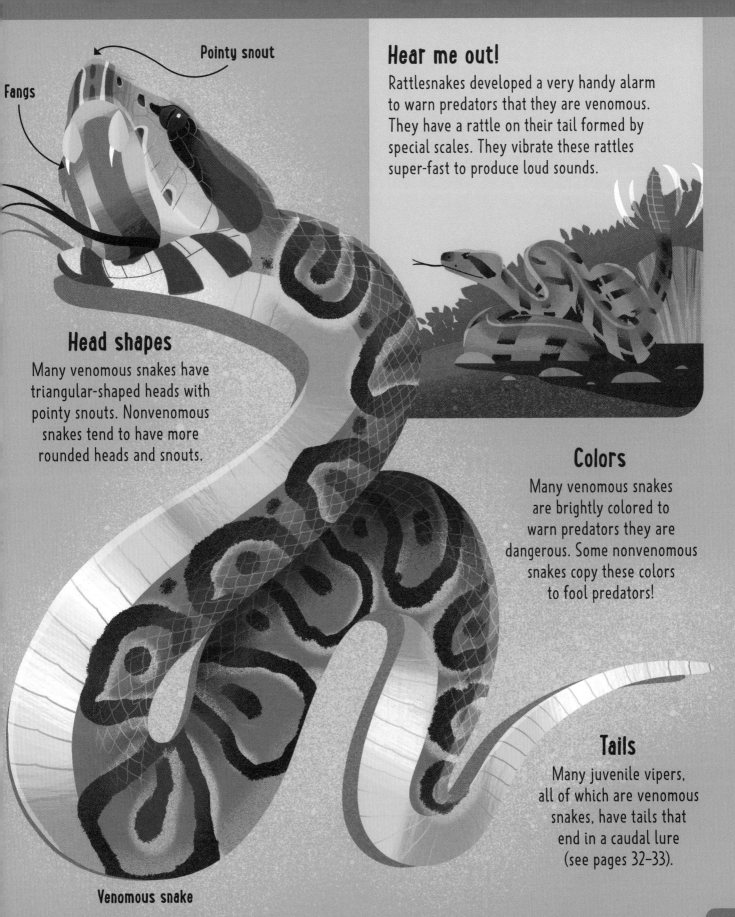

Fangs

Pointy snout

Hear me out!

Rattlesnakes developed a very handy alarm to warn predators that they are venomous. They have a rattle on their tail formed by special scales. They vibrate these rattles super-fast to produce loud sounds.

Head shapes

Many venomous snakes have triangular-shaped heads with pointy snouts. Nonvenomous snakes tend to have more rounded heads and snouts.

Colors

Many venomous snakes are brightly colored to warn predators they are dangerous. Some nonvenomous snakes copy these colors to fool predators!

Tails

Many juvenile vipers, all of which are venomous snakes, have tails that end in a caudal lure (see pages 32–33).

Venomous snake

HISSSSSS

Playing dead to stay alive

It's a cloudy and cool afternoon in South Carolina, USA, and an eastern hognose snake is slithering through a meadow. Like all snakes, he tries to **avoid confrontation** with animals and humans, but things don't always go according to plan... Suddenly, our snake becomes aware of a fox approaching him. The fox probably thinks it has stumbled upon an easy meal, but the eastern hognose snake is determined to prove it wrong. In an attempt to scare off the predator, the snake puffs up and flattens his neck like a cobra!

To his despair, this threatening display doesn't work. But that's okay—this snake has a **secret weapon**. Just as the fox goes to bite his tail, the eastern hognose flips around violently on his back, opens his mouth, and releases a foul odor. It looks like the snake has died! Puzzled, the fox decides it no longer wants to eat the dead snake and trots away. Once the coast is clear, the snake slithers to safety!

A close escape

In the humid jungles of Indonesia, in Southeast Asia, lives a snake called the paradise flying snake. Can you possibly guess what its special skill is? This particular snake is relaxing on a tree branch when she spots movement out of the corner of her eye. It's a **bird of prey**—and it's heading her way! The snake needs to escape, and quick.

The flying snake **leaps off** the tree! As she falls, she flattens her body and begins to glide through the sky.

After a few seconds in the air, the snake lands in a new tree. But she's not in the clear yet... She uses her climbing abilities to quickly hide before the bird can find her again. Snakes have developed many unique ways to escape predators but there aren't many more impressive than these reptilian pilots!

A master of disguise

Perfectly camouflaged against the rocks of Iran in Western Asia lies one of the most impressive tricksters in the animal kingdom—the spider-tailed horned viper. In a harsh climate like this, the viper has no room for error when it comes to catching prey: any wrong moves and she could starve to death. For this reason, she has a unique adaptation on her tail called a **caudal lure**, which she uses to trick and catch prey. Spotting a hungry bird flying by, the viper sets the trap. Staying as still as she can, she wiggles her caudal lure. From the bird's point of view, it looks just like a spider moving across the rocks!

Different species have different caudal lures depending on what kind of prey they eat.

Sensing an easy meal, the bird dives down and bites what it thinks is the spider. Big mistake! The viper **strikes** and secures her meal.

Many snakes have a caudal lure as babies to help them catch prey, but they slowly lose it as they grow older, a bit like training wheels on a bicycle. Spider-tailed horned vipers are lucky—they keep them their whole lives!

Meanwhile... The anaconda has found a nice spot where she can begin digesting the caiman. She will remain almost completely still for up to four months!

33

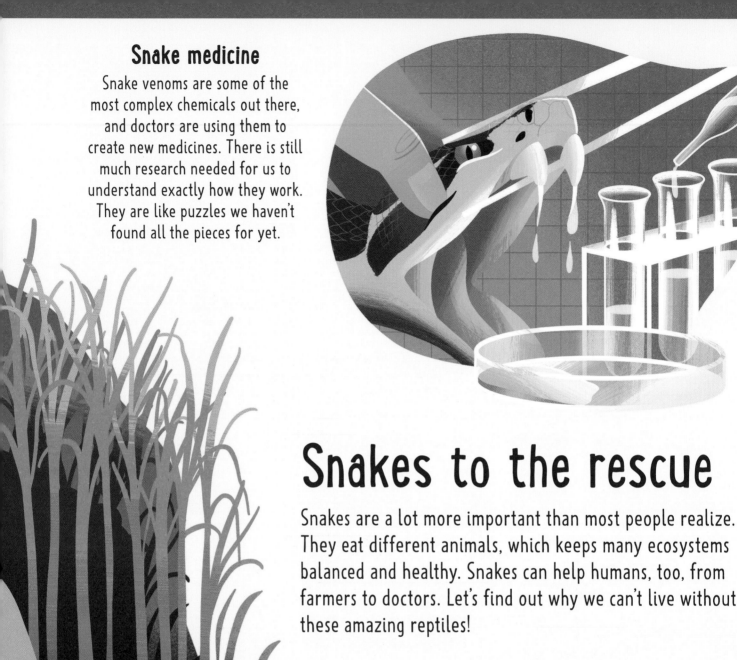

Snake medicine

Snake venoms are some of the most complex chemicals out there, and doctors are using them to create new medicines. There is still much research needed for us to understand exactly how they work. They are like puzzles we haven't found all the pieces for yet.

Snakes to the rescue

Snakes are a lot more important than most people realize. They eat different animals, which keeps many ecosystems balanced and healthy. Snakes can help humans, too, from farmers to doctors. Let's find out why we can't live without these amazing reptiles!

Pest control

Snakes help farmers by eating rodents. Rodents destroy crops and can spread diseases. Without snakes, rodent numbers would grow too large and entire farms would be at risk.

Snakes on the menu

Even though snakes have a reputation for being vicious predators, they also serve an important role by being prey for other animals. Many mammals, birds, reptiles, amphibians, and even fish rely on snakes as food. They are a crucial part of the food chain!

Snakes aren't fussy eaters. In fact, some snakes even eat other snakes!

Snake-eaters

Snakes don't just keep other animal populations in check, they also control other snake species. Take kingsnakes and king cobras for example—their prey of choice? Snakes!

Fighting for love

As the sun begins to lower in the sky, the stage is set for an epic battle. The two male timber rattlesnakes who encountered each other earlier have now **caught the attention** of a curious spectator: it's a female timber rattlesnake! Can you see her spying on them?

Finding a mate is the main goal for male snakes, which creates a lot of competition. Both of these rattlesnakes have lethal venom, so biting is not a safe option. Instead, they **wrestle** to see who can pin the other's head down! This match lasts a long time because both of these rattlers are superstrong. Eventually one snake smashes the other to the ground with a thud and the battle is over. The winning snake gets the girl, while the loser slithers off to search for love elsewhere!

Thud!

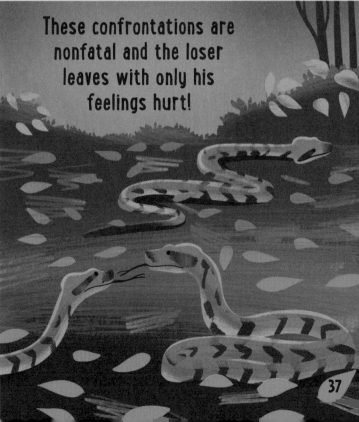

These confrontations are nonfatal and the loser leaves with only his feelings hurt!

Keeping cozy

In the snowy forests of Scandinavia you wouldn't expect to find many snakes or reptiles, but the European adder is a bit of an outlier. Unlike most snakes, he can survive **freezing temperatures**. To do so, he has a few tricks up his sleeve.

This European adder was born with a fat reserve that acted like a winter coat when he was young. But now that he's all grown-up, he must find other ways to keep warm. One method for surviving these cold months is by using animal burrows as dens. A den is like a cozy **winter cabin** for the adder to escape the harsh temperatures. Luckily he finds one just in time before it starts to snow heavily. And he has some company! Other European adders are gathered here in this burrow to conserve their body heat.

On warmer days, our snake will come out of the den to **thermoregulate**, soaking up heat from the sun. But for now, the warmth of his friends will keep him safe.

The European adder is the only snake in the world found north of the Arctic Circle.

Surfing and hunting

Can you guess where the yellow-lipped sea krait gets his name from? If you guessed that it's because of his yellow lips and the fact that he lives underwater, bingo! Think of him as the supercool surfer dude of the snake world. He is well-equipped for ocean life. He has a **paddle-like tail** to swim through the coral reefs he calls home, and he can hold his breath for up to 30 minutes. This evening, he's on the hunt. This krait has fancy tastes and simple fish will not do, so a moray eel is on the menu! The eel is hiding in the reef, but this isn't a problem for the skilled krait—his slim body allows him to slide through the small gaps with ease.

The yellow-lipped
sea krait lives in
the Indian and
Pacific oceans.

Meanwhile... The eastern indigo snake has fully shed his skin and is now sliding back into the gopher tortoise burrow. Here he will stay warm during cold temperatures at night.

When the krait finds the right moment to attack, the **underwater battle** begins! Moray eels have sharp teeth that make them dangerous prey, so the krait needs to subdue his foe quickly.

Before the eel can strike, the krait sinks his fangs into the eel's skin and injects venom. It makes the eel unable to move. Mission accomplished!

Ready to face the world

The moon is high in the sky in the Indian rainforest where the female king cobra has been tending her eggs. As the eggs are about to hatch, she abandons the nest—her job is done! Suddenly a few of the eggs **start to move**. The baby snakes are ready to take their first breaths! The young snakes hatch out of their eggs and begin to slither away all by themselves. Just like their mother, they are extremely venomous. The only difference is that they're much smaller.

No snakes feed or nurture their young, and only a few defend their eggs before they hatch, like the king cobra mother did. For all snakes, it is a tough world out there from the minute they are born. As adults, king cobras are some of the most dangerous snakes in the world, but the small baby cobras are easy food for many animals. They will have to be careful and smart for years until they become **rulers of the jungle** like their mother. Sadly, few of these babies will live that long. but the ones that do will be the toughest and wisest cobras of them all!

10PM The future of medicine

It's a warm night in Alabama, USA, and a copperhead snake is going about his evening as usual when he's suddenly approached by a human. Thankfully this isn't a hiker or a hunter—it's a **snake biologist** on a mission! The biologist carefully uses a snake hook to catch the copperhead. The snake is a venomous pit viper so careful handling is a must.

After successfully picking up the viper behind his head, the biologist gets him to bite into a cup. The venom flows into it and is safely collected. The biologist is going to take this copperhead venom back to the lab.

She is researching potential **treatments for cancer**, and this venom might just be the key ingredient. Venoms are also used to make antivenoms to cure people who are bitten by venomous snakes.

Once the biologist has everything she needs, she lets the copperhead go back **into the wild** where he belongs. He quickly slithers away into the night, completely unharmed.

Meanwhile... After escaping the bird of prey, the paradise flying snake is now safely sleeping high up in a tree.

Extracting venom from snakes is called "snake milking."

Glossary

Camouflage
A form of disguise used by animals to blend into their environment, typically used to hide from predators or to hunt prey.

Constriction
A method that some snakes use to kill prey. They squeeze an animal's airway until it can no longer breathe.

Ecdysis
The process of reptiles getting rid of their old skin. Also known as shedding.

Ecosystem
A collection of animals, plants, and organisms that live in the same area and interact with each other.

Ectotherm
A cold-blooded animal whose internal temperature is dependent on external sources of heat. It uses the sun or heated rocks to maintain its body temperature.

Fang
A long, hollow grooved tooth that injects venom when striking prey. Venomous snakes have fangs, but nonvenomous snakes do not.

Heat pit
The holes that some snakes have on their face that contain heat receptors. They allow snakes to detect warm-blooded animals.

Predator
An animal that hunts and eats other animals.

Prey
An animal that is eaten by another animal.

Reptiles
A group of cold-blooded animals with scaly skin that lay eggs. Snakes, lizards, turtles, tortoises, alligators, and crocodiles are all reptiles.

Scales
A special type of skin that forms a protective shield over an animal's body.

Thermoregulation
The ability of animals to keep their internal temperature stable regardless of what the outside temperature is.

Venom
The toxin produced by venomous animals that is used to hurt prey or predators. Venom is administered through bites, stings, or scratches.

Vertebrae
Small bones that are connected and form a backbone.

Index

Species list

Snake anatomy:
Lampropeltis triangulum

7AM: *Drymarchon couperi*
8AM: *Eunectes murinus*
9AM: *Malayopython reticulatus*
10AM: *Pituophis melanoleucus*

Snake families:
Viperidae: *Bothriechis schlegelii*
Colubridae: *Drymarchon couperi*
Pythonidae: *Malayopython reticulatus*
Elapidae: *Ophiophagus hannah*
Boidae: *Eunectes murinus*

11AM: *Eunectes murinus*
12PM: *Oxyuranus microlepidotus*
1PM: *Ophiophagus hannah*
2PM: *Drymarchon couperi*

Venomous or nonvenomous?
Venomous: *Agkistrodon piscivorous*
Nonvenomous: *Nerodia sipedon*

3PM: *Heterodon platirhinos*
4PM: *Chrysopelea paradisi*
5PM: *Pseudocerastes urarachnoides*

Snakes to the rescue:
Top left: *Crotalus oreganus*
Bottom left: *Oxyuranus scutellatus*
Top right: *Ophiophagus hannah*
Bottom right: *Lampropeltis getula &
Agkistrodon piscivorous*

6PM: *Crotalus horridus*
7PM: *Vipera berus*
8PM: *Laticauda colubrina*
9PM: *Ophiophagus hannah*
10PM: *Agkistrodon contortrix*

This has been a

NEON SQUID
production

To my dad and mom for investing in my passions for science and expressing myself in the arts growing up.

To my brothers, Joel and Robert, and little sis, Angelle, for always encouraging me.

To Bobby, Conner, and Micaiah for being the best friends (brothers) ever.

Genesis 1:26

Author: Christian Cave
Illustrator: Rebecca Mills

Editorial Assistant: Malu Rocha
Designer: Clare Joyce
US Editor: Jill Freshney
Proofreader: Laura Gilbert

Copyright © 2024 St. Martin's Press
120 Broadway, New York, NY 10271

Created for St. Martin's Press
by Neon Squid
The Stables, 4 Crinan Street,
London, N1 9XW

EU representative: Macmillan
Publishers Ireland Ltd,
1st Floor, The Liffey Trust Centre,
117–126 Sheriff Street Upper,
Dublin 1, D01 YC43

10 9 8 7 6 5 4 3 2 1

Library of Congress Cataloging-in-Publication Data is available.

Printed and bound in Guangdong, China by Leo Paper Products Ltd.

ISBN: 978-1-684-49360-9

Published in April 2024.

www.neonsquidbooks.com